Better Homes and Gardens®

LOOK UP, UP, UP

Hi! My name is Max.
I have some great projects
to show you—and they're all about
looking up at the sky! We're going
to have lots of fun making
them together.

Inside You'll Find...

Search the night sky for constellations.

Star Pictures

Max and his best friend, Elliot, enjoy watching for the first star of the night. They like to make a special wish on it. Go ahead. Try wishing on a twinkling star tonight.

Did you know...

● A long time ago, the people who studied the stars gave them names. These star watchers imagined the groups of stars made pictures that looked like animals and sometimes even people. These groups of stars are called constellations (con-stuh-LAY-shuns). Can you say that?

● Max and Elliot like to look up at the night sky when it's full of stars. They search the sky for the star

pictures. Can you find the cat, rabbit, lamb, fish, and skunk?

● Just as there is no one else quite like you, no two stars are exactly alike. Some stars are brighter, some are bigger, and some are yellow, or red, or blue, or white.

● There's even one star that you can't see at night. Do you know which one it is? It's our sun! The sun is called a daytime star.

A glitter-and-glue craft.

Twinkling Glitter Stars

Create pretty stars that sparkle like those in the night sky. Hang the Glitter Stars from your bedroom ceiling. Then when you're lying down, you can look up at them.

What you'll need...

- White crafts glue (select one that dries hard)
- Waxed paper
- Glitter in assorted colors

1 Use a bottle of glue with a pointed tip to draw a star shape on a piece of waxed paper (see photo). The glue lines need to be thick and wide.

2 Sprinkle the glue with glitter (see photo). Make sure it completely covers the glue. Let the star dry for 2 days.

3 Remove the excess glitter and save for another time. Carefully peel the waxed paper away from your Glitter Stars, working gently in from each point (see photo).

A healthful fruit salad for hungry space trekkers.

Rocket Ship Salad

3, 2, 1 ... Blast off! This fun-to-make and yummy-in-the-tummy fruit salad is great for refueling when you're running low on energy.

What you'll need...

- 1 large banana
- Table knife
- 1 slice pineapple
- ½ cup cottage cheese
- Measuring cup

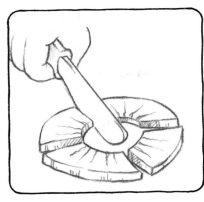

1 Peel the banana. Cut the banana in half crosswise. This makes 2 pieces.

2 Cut the slice of pineapple into quarters. This makes 4 pieces.

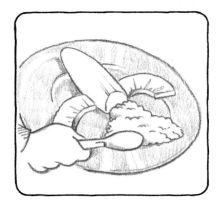

3 For each salad, place a banana half on a plate. Place 2 pineapple quarters near the base of each banana. Spoon ¼ cup of the cottage cheese around the bottom to look like rocket exhaust.

Elliot, would you like half of my banana?

Max, please take two of my pineapple quarters.

The banana is divided in half. Max writes one-half like this: ½.

The pineapple slice is divided into quarters. Elliot writes one-quarter like this: ¼.

An easy balloon project that moves on air power.

Shoot-for-the-Moon Balloons

Count down hours of fun with your very own balloon rocket. Let your balloon loose to see how high it flies. You're the pilot!

What you'll need...

- Plastic drinking straw
- Scissors
- Stapler
- Tape
- 1 egg cup, cut from an egg carton
- Balloon
- Pencil

1 Cut the straw in half. Reserve one half for another use.

2 Staple the straw in the middle along its length.

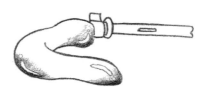

3 Tightly tape balloon to one end of the straw.

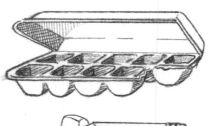

4 Use the sharpened end of a pencil to make a hole in the bottom of egg cup.

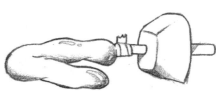

5 Push the open end of the straw through the hole up to the tape.

6 Now blow through the open end of the straw to inflate. Let it go.

Look up here! Look up there!
Look as high as you dare.
Look as far as you might.
Have fun, Max! Hang on tight!

Food coloring bursts into a colorful display.

Food-Coloring Fireworks

Why wait for the Fourth of July to watch the fireworks up in the sky? Plain white paper bursts into beautiful bright colors when you make Food-Coloring Fireworks.

What you'll need...

- Newspapers or brown kraft paper
- White paper or construction paper
- Food coloring
- Plastic drinking straw

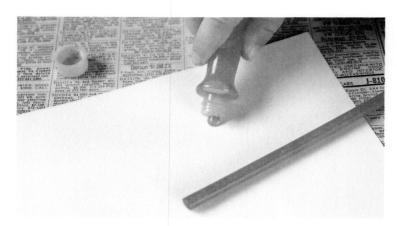

1 Cover your work surface with newspapers. Place white paper on the newspapers. Put a large drop of food coloring in the center of the white paper (see photo).

2 Holding one end of the straw above the drop of coloring, blow through the other end of the straw (see photo). How hard you blow determines how far and how fast the drop of coloring moves.

   After you've blown the first drop of coloring as far as you want, do the same with more drops of color.

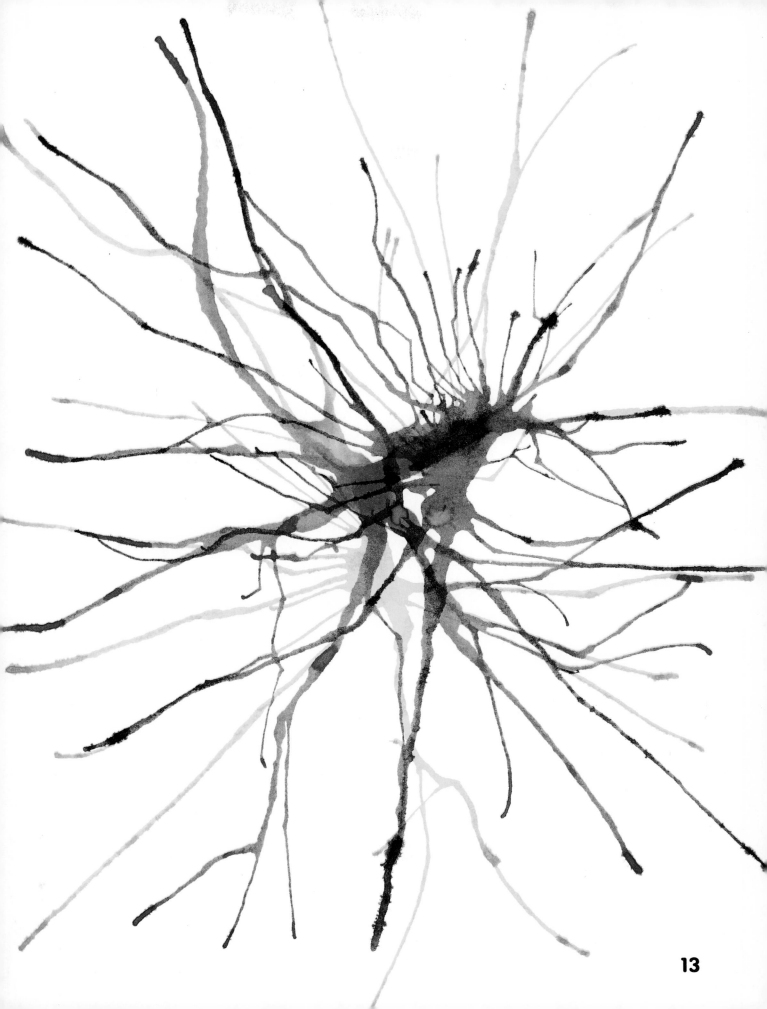

Busy Buzzing Bees

Oh, no! There's a bee on Max's nose! Where is the other bee that matches the one looking at Max? Can you point to the other bees that look alike?

Bees

Busy Buzzers

A worker bee keeps busy,
   And always does its best.
When a bee is on a flower blossom,
   It can't stop to smell the rest.
Do you ever wonder what it is,
   These busy buzzers do?
Well, they're making lots of honey,
   Just to sweeten me and you.

Did you know...

● A honeybee has four wings—two on each side of its body. Like all other insects, a bee has six legs (three pairs).

● A bee has two large eyes in the front of its head, and three small eyes on top. Imagine that! Every bee has six legs and five eyes. How many legs and eyes do you have?

● A bee has antennae (an-TEN-i). Can you say that? Antennae stick out of the bee's head. They are for smelling and feeling—that's why they're sometimes called feelers.

● A honeybee has a stinger in its tail. This is the only way a bee has to protect itself and its family. Max knows he shouldn't bother bees, because a bee sting hurts a lot.

Now that you know what a bee looks like, why don't you draw a picture of one? Remember to put black stripes on its body.

A nutritious peanut butter snack.

Honeybees

Buzz into your kitchen to make a swarm of yummy honeybees. Making this fun-to-eat snack will keep you busy as a bee.

What you'll need...

- Measuring cups
- Measuring spoons
- ½ cup peanut butter
- 1 tablespoon honey
- ⅓ cup nonfat dry milk
- 2 tablespoons sesame seed
- 2 tablespoons toasted wheat germ
- Unsweetened cocoa powder
- Sliced almonds
- Mixing bowl
- Wooden spoon
- Waxed paper
- Tray
- Toothpick

1 With adult help, first measure all the food. For the dough, in a mixing bowl use the wooden spoon to stir together peanut butter and honey. Stir in nonfat dry milk, sesame seed, and wheat germ till well mixed (see photo).

2 Lay a piece of waxed paper on a tray. For the bee body, shape 1 teaspoonful of dough into an oval. Place it on the tray (see photo).

3 Dip a toothpick into the cocoa powder and press it gently across the top of the bee body. This makes the stripes.
  Stick sliced almonds in the sides for wings (see photo). Chill bees in the refrigerator for 30 minutes. Makes about 28 bees.

Search for the hidden birds.

Up in a Tree

Go outside and look up at the trees. Notice how some trees are taller and bigger than others. Some even have fruit or nuts. And some are a home to birds. Can you help Max find the 6 hidden birds in the tree?

Did you know...

● While a tree is growing above the ground, it's also growing below the ground. The part that's above the ground is called a trunk and it may have many branches. Roots grow underground to help make the tree strong and sturdy.

● A tree needs air to become big and beautiful. It uses the leaves and the many cracks in its branches to breathe.

● A tree gets thirsty and needs water to drink. The tree roots get water from the soil and then the tree grows taller.

● You can find out about how old a tree is just by measuring its trunk with a tape measure. Usually a tree grows one inch bigger around each year. So, if a tree's trunk measurement is 15 inches around, then it's 15 years old. Measure your favorite tree.

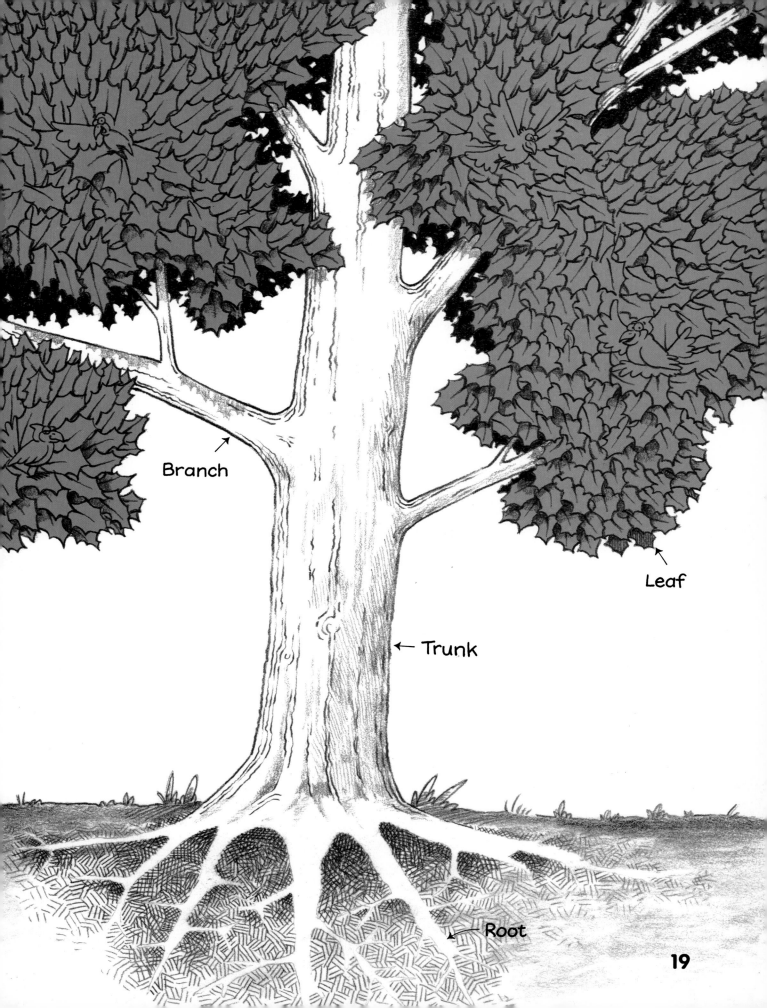

Branch

Leaf

Trunk

Root

Construction-paper pinwheels for indoors or out.

Whirlie Birds

What makes Whirlie Birds whirl? You do. Blow on their wings or wave them through the air like Max is doing.

What you'll need...

- One 4x5-inch piece of construction paper
- Pencil
- Scissors
- Tape

- Crayons or colored pencils
- One 4x4-inch piece of construction paper

- Ruler
- Pencil with eraser or a drinking straw
- Thumbtack

 **1** For the bird body, fold the 4x5-inch piece of paper lengthwise in half. Draw a bird outline along folded edge.

 **2** Cut out the bird body. Use small pieces of tape to close the unfolded edge. Decorate your bird with crayons.

 **3** Tape the eraser end of the pencil to the back of the bird body; set aside.

 **4** Draw lines to connect the opposite corners of the 4x4-inch piece of paper. Where the lines cross, draw a small ½-inch square.

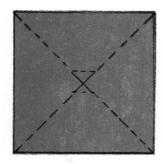

5 Cut along dotted lines (as shown). Remove the 2 opposite triangles.

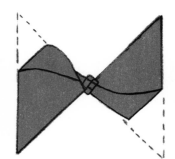

6 For the bird wings, bring the opposite points of the 2 triangles to the small square in the center (as shown). Attach with tape.

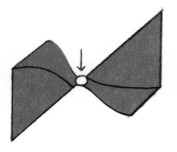

7 Push thumbtack through the center of small square. The wings will spin more easily if the hole is a bit larger than the tack.

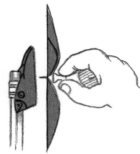

8 Attach the bird wings, with the flat side toward the bird body, by pushing the tack into the pencil eraser. Now blow!

A simple yet amazing nature craft.

Leaf Rubbings

Leave it to the leaves to make a good impression. They're just waiting for you to make them show up on paper.

What you'll need...

- Tree leaves
- Tape
- Paper
- Crayons or colored pencils

1 Tape leaf stem to the work surface (see photo). Make sure the leaf is flat and that its back, or vein side, is up.

Lay a piece of paper over the leaf. Tape corners to the counter. This keeps the paper from moving.

2 Firmly rub the crayon over the leaf. Watch as the leaf pattern appears on the paper.

No-fuss fruit turnovers made from purchased pastry.

Pies in the Sky

Do pies grow on trees? No, but the fruit for yummy pies does.
Can you find an apple, a pear, and a peach in the picture?

What you'll need...

- Fruit filling (see page 32)
- Measuring cup
- Pastry rectangles (see page 32)
- Milk
- Table fork
- Baking pan
- Sugar

1 For each pie, place about ⅓ cup of the fruit filling on half of the pastry rectangle. Moisten the edges of the pastry with a little milk. Fold the pastry over fruit (see photo).

2 Use a table fork to seal the edge of each pie. This keeps the filling from leaking out. Be careful not to tear a hole in the pastry.

3 Place the pies on a greased 15x10x1-inch baking pan. Use a table fork to make small holes in each top. This keeps the pastry from getting soggy during baking. Brush tops with a little milk and sprinkle lightly with some sugar.

Bake as directed on page 32.

Look Up, Look Down

One fine day, Max was outside flying his kite. What did he see when he looked up into the sky? What did Max see when he looked down? Can you point to the squares, circles, triangles, and rectangles in the picture?

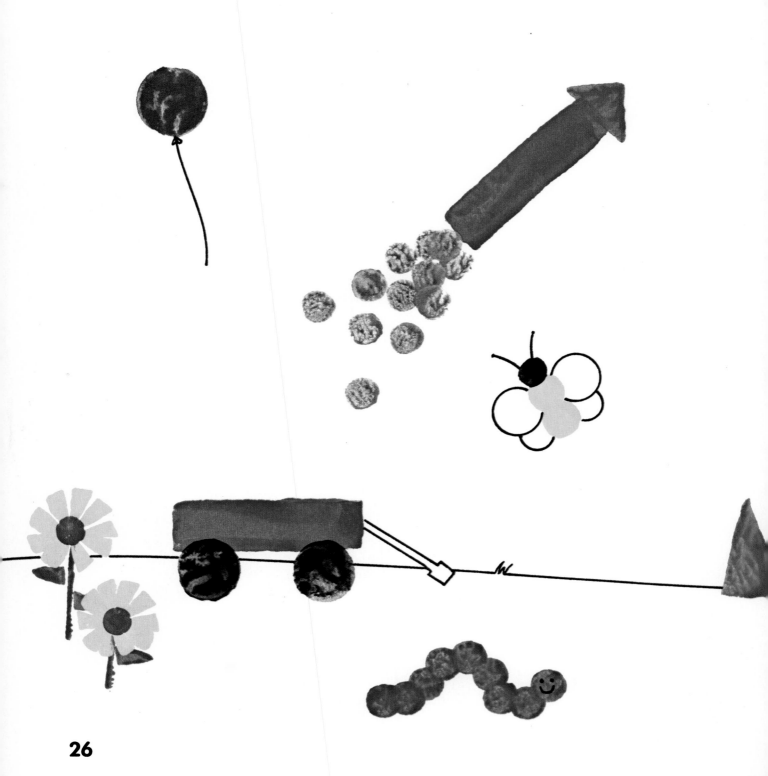

Printing Presses

Max is getting ready to print a picture. Did you know you could make a picture using a cork? Or a sponge? Or even a piece of carrot? They make great printing stamps!

What you'll need...
- Tempera paints
- Jar lids
- Corks or stamps (see opposite)
- White paper or construction paper

1 Pour small amounts of the tempera paint colors into the jar lids.

2 Dip the end of the cork lightly into the paint.

3 Press the cork onto the paper to make your picture.

Anything Goes

Half the fun of printing is experimenting with various shapes (opposite). And, the designs are limited only by your imagination. Turn your artwork into great gifts like note cards, stationery, and decorative gift wrap.

Square

Objects that make
a square stamp:
● Sponge, cut into
any size.
● Art gum eraser.

Circle

Objects that make
a circular stamp:
● Carrot piece.
● Thread spool.
● Pencil eraser.

Triangle

Objects that make
a triangular stamp:
● Art gum eraser
or square sponge,
cut diagonally.

Rectangle

Objects that make
a rectangular stamp:
● Sponge, cut into
any size.
● Art gum eraser.

29

Parents' Pages

We've filled this special section with more activities, recipes, reading suggestions, hints we learned from our kid-testers, and many other helpful tips.

Star Pictures

See pages 4 and 5

For thousands of years, star-gazers have been gazing into the night sky. You and your kids can see the constellations on any clear night. On a summer night, lie down on a blanket with your kids. Let them imagine animals or people.

Or, inside your house, turn the ceiling into a star-filled sky. With a pencil, make a hole for each star on the bottom of a plastic cup. In a dark room, let your children shine a flashlight into the cup. The points of light on the ceiling will look like stars in the sky.

● Reading suggestions:
*Half a Moon
and One Whole Star*
   by Crescent Dragonwagon
The Sky Is Full of Stars
   by Franklyn M. Branley

Twinkling Glitter Stars

See pages 6 and 7

This project is so simple that even our youngest kid-testers didn't need much help. And if stars are too tricky, your young artists may like making their own shapes.

In just a few minutes, your kids can glue and glitter dozens of stars for your family's Christmas or Fourth of July decorating. You can hang their bright and shiny Glitter Stars in a window or tie them to a wire hanger for a mobile.

Rocket Ship Salad

See pages 8 and 9

Turn your children's mealtime into an exciting space adventure by serving them Rocket Ship Salad. And set the scene this way:

"As a young, aspiring space trekker from this universe, you'll be eager to discover the powerful energy source in Rocket Ship Salad.

"Your mission is...
● To explore exciting new foods.
● To seek out new tastes and new experiences.
● To boldly try everything on your plates.
● To grow strong and prosper!"

Ask your children if they can think of more challenges. It's a great way to teach them good attitudes toward eating.

Shoot-for-the-Moon Balloons

See pages 10 and 11

Do your children know that astronauts ride in a rocket ship? Help them transform a cardboard box into a rocket ship, and let them decorate it.

Ask your children:
● Where would they go in their rocket ship?
● What would they take with them for their space trip?
● What would they find when they visited the moon?
● Reading suggestions:
Papa, Please Get the Moon for Me by Eric Carle
Mooncake by Frank Asch

Food-Coloring Fireworks

See pages 12 and 13

There are advantages to letting your children paint with food coloring. If they knock over the bottle, the food coloring won't spill. And, the small plastic food coloring bottles are perfect for little hands to squeeze.

Watching fireworks, whatever your age, is exciting. The Chinese, invented them more than 800 years ago. Have your children ever seen fireworks? If so, ask them:
● What did they like most?
● Did they "ooh and aah" at the bright lights and the showers of dazzling sparks?
● Did they like the smoke and noise?
● Did they know fireworks are small rockets that are shot up into the night sky?

Busy Buzzing Bees

See pages 14 and 15

Most kids are fascinated to hear about bees making honey and living in a hive. They might enjoy a field trip to visit a beekeeper. Or, check with your city's zoo or science center. They often have a bee colony on display.

Honeybees

See pages 16 and 17

Our kid-testers turned into worker bees when it was time to make this snack. They enjoyed shaping the bee bodies, making the cocoa powder stripes, and putting on the almond wings. But it was the honey-peanut flavor that kept the children buzzing around for more.

Honey and honey products are safe foods for anyone over one year old. Remember, never feed honey or honey products to infants less than one year old. Some honey contains a bacterium that has been linked to infant botulism, an acute poisoning.
● Reading suggestions:
Here Come the Bees!
by Alice E. Goudey
Close-Up of a Honeybee
by Virgil E. Foster

Up in a Tree

See pages 18 and 19

By decorating a tree in your yard for winter-feeding birds, your children can take part in an age-old Swedish tradition that began in Stockholm.

Help your children to adorn a tree with some treats: beef suet, a popped corn and fresh cranberry garland, carrot slices, marshmallows, stale bread, orange slices, and stale doughnuts.

Once birds find food at your house, they'll expect to continue finding it there. So, if your children start feeding the birds in the winter, they shouldn't stop until spring comes.

Whirlie Birds

See pages 20 and 21

Talk to your children about wind as moving air. Your kids can blow like the wind. Ask them to create wind by blowing softly on their Whirlie Birds' wings. Now ask them to blow harder.

Go outdoors. Have your children hold the Whirlie Birds up. Is there enough wind to move the wings? Now have your children wave the Whirlie Birds through the air. Is there a difference in how fast the wings move?

Explain to your kids that the wind blows every day—some days hard and other days soft. Do they like it when the wind blows softly through their hair? Ask them to draw a picture of a very windy day.

Leaf Rubbings

See pages 22 and 23

Making leaf rubbings with all kinds of leaves helps your children learn that each type makes its own unique design.

Leaves aren't the only objects you can use for rubbings. Take a look around your house. Things such as coins, keys, paper clips, twine, ribbon, or paper doilies are common items that are fun to use.

Pies in the Sky

See pages 24 and 25

Kids in the kitchen! Please, don't despair. With a little organization, teaching kids to cook can be fun for all.

Pies in the Sky

- 1 15-ounce package 9-inch folded refrigerated unbaked piecrust (2 crusts)
- 1 large apple, or 2 medium peaches or pears
- 2 tablespoons brown sugar
- ¼ teaspoon ground cinnamon
- ⅛ teaspoon ground nutmeg
      Milk
      Sugar

- For the pastry rectangles, bring the piecrusts to room temperature according to the package directions. Unfold the piecrusts; peel off one plastic sheet as directed.
- Trim each piecrust circle

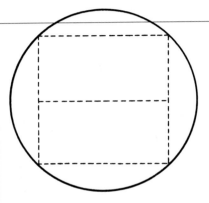

into an 8-inch square. Cut each square in half to form a total of 4 rectangles.
- For the fruit filling, thoroughly rinse and peel the fruit. Cut fruit in half; remove and discard the core or pit from the fruit. Chop fruit. Set aside.
- In a small bowl stir together brown sugar, cinnamon, and nutmeg. Stir in chopped fruit; coat well. Continue as directed on page 24.
- Bake the pies in a 425° oven for 18 to 20 minutes or till golden brown. Transfer the pies to a wire cooling rack. Serve warm or cool. Makes 4.

Look Up, Look Down

See pages 26 and 27

Encourage your children to understand and name opposites. Here are a few to get you and your children started:
- First and last.
- Over and under.
- In and out.
- Top and bottom.
- Short and tall.
   Try to think of some more.

Recognizing shapes is one of the first skills young children accomplish. Ask them to find items in your home that have square, rectangular, circular, and triangular shapes.

Printing Presses

See pages 28 and 29

Because vegetables and fruits grow in a variety of sizes, shapes, and textures, they are perfect for print making.

We learned an important tip during our kid-testing. At least one hour before you start the printing project, allow the cut vegetables and fruits to dry on paper towels. The paint will stick to the cut surfaces better, making printing easier.

Here are a few suggestions that make interesting prints:
- Radish half: Leave a piece of root to give a "stem" print.
- Mushroom half: The hollow stems create outlines.
- Apple, halved crosswise: Remove the seeds for a star print.
- Cauliflower: A small piece looks like a little tree.

Radish   Mushroom

Apple   Cauliflower

BETTER HOMES AND GARDENS. BOOKS
Editor: Gerald M. Knox
Art Director: Ernest Shelton
Managing Editor: David Kirchner
Department Head, Food and Family Life: Sharyl Heiken

LOOK UP, UP, UP
Editors: Sandra Granseth and Martha Schiel
Editorial Project Manager: Rosanne Weber Mattson
Graphic Designers: Linda Ford Vermie and Brian Wignall
Contributing Illustrator: Buck Jones
Contributing Photographer: Scott Little